Navigation

by Brittney Corrigan

*for Sue~
May you always
find your way.
B
2012*

The Habit of Rainy Nights Press
Portland, Oregon

© 2012, Brittney Corrigan
all rights reserved

1st Printing

Acknowledgments:
With thanks to the following publications in which
some of the poems in this collection previously appeared:

The Hayden's Ferry Review: "Constellations"
The Texas Observer: "Aqueducts" and "The Navigator's Triangle"
Borderlands: Texas Poetry Review: "Expectations"
The Blue Mesa Review: "In the Name"
What Have You Lost? (Greenwillow Books): "Aqueducts"
Many Mountains Moving: "Messengers"
The Oregon Review: "Sunday Mornings"
Stringtown: "Islands"
Manzanita Quarterly: "Sky Falling" and "Nests"
The Autism Trail Guide (Future Horizons): "Signs"
Hyperlexia: "Echolalia," "Sensory Profile," and "Hollows"
Untitled Country Review: "Aviary"
Poetic Medicine: "Architecture"
YB: "Visiting Lighthouses"
Quick Lucks: "Everything"
Halfway Down the Stairs: "Cold"
Cider Press Review: "Fox Pieces, Orcas Island"

And with gratitude to Soapstone: A Writing Retreat for Women for the residency that allowed me the time to write some of these poems.

Cover image credit: Victor Emert
Author photo credit: Serena Davidson
Book design: Duane Poncy

The Habit of Rainy Nights Press,
an imprint of Elohi Gadugi
Portland, Oregon
http://rainynightspress.org

Navigation

For Perry Weissman,
one of the people on whom nothing is lost.

CONTENTS

I.   The Mapmakers

Aqueducts 6
Constellations 8
The Navigator's Triangle 10
In Tunnels Full of Wings 12
Grandmother's Italian 14
The Engine 16
For My Sister, Who Has Epilepsy 18
Good Road Woman 20
Fox Pieces, Orcas Island 22
Funeral 23
Ceremony 24
Crow Visitors 26
Birds of Passage 28

II.   Sighting the Land

Imagining Loons 34
Denver's Rain 36
Leaving A House 38
Landscape 40
Letter in a Flood 42
Visiting Lighthouses 43
Nests 44
Birdwatching 45
Islands 46
Driving to the San Juans 48
Construction 49
This Anniversary, I Am in San Francisco 50
Wind River 51
Architecture 52
Housewarming 53

III. Uncharted Worlds

The Day After Finding Out My Sister is Pregnant 56
At Six Months 57
Messengers 58
Everything 60
Weather Conditions 61
Three Days 62
Yoga as a Mother 64
Faith as a Mother 66
Small Talk 67
Echolalia 69
Sensory Profile 70
Hollows 72
Signs 73
Dipper 75
What They Won't See 76

IV. Journeys & Returns

Wind Horses 80
Travel 81
Inside 83
Cold 84
Expectations 85
Aviary 87
Crows 88
St. Mark's Cathedral, Seattle 89
Sunday Mornings 91
Angels 92
That Quickly 93
Sky Falling 95
Scotch Broom 97
In The Name 99
Massage 101
Window 102
How We Come Home 103

The Mapmakers

*Remember that you are all people
and that all people are you.*

JOY HARJO

Aqueducts

I have carried water
to bed with me every night
since I was able to tip a cup
to my lips with my own small hands,
adopted a cup as my own
for years at a time until
it was broken or lost—
though it was not the cup that mattered
so much as the holding of water,
the water keeping watch over the night.

Two centuries back, my grandmother's ancestors
built the aqueducts in Turin, Italy.
My mother tells me this today,
and it is the only thing I know of them—
the family *Audo*—a line sunk
by the weight of my great grandfather
Grosso —a name as vast
and still as the bowl of a reservoir.
The names of my great grandparents—
Celestina, Anton—are as far back
as I can name, as my mother can name.
The stories come to me slowly, as water
struggling to pass through a dam.

I know a few small things—like switchbacking
up a hill: that Celestina came to America first,
her hands empty of pennies and English—
that my grandmother refuses to speak
her native tongue, does not speak at all
of her life before my grandfather, the war navigator,
the architect of her world, who washed over
her family name like a flood.

I imagine the aqueducts of Northern Italy—
pressed into the landscape by my family's hands,
climbing into the city like children
into laps, reaching for my grandmother's face
with small-boned hands: the hands my mother
used to raise me above her head, the hands
in which I carry water—holding it to my lips
in the dark, night after night.

Constellations

My mother learned that bear claws
were made of stars and sword hilts
were made of stars and cooking pots
were full of stars and w's were drawn
with stars

from my grandfather, who once
was a navigator and pointed
the way to where the bombs were dropped.

My mother learned words like
  Ursa Minor
  Orion
  Cassiopeia
the way other children learn phonics:
stars like syllables dancing
on my grandfather's teeth
and spilling from my grandfather's tongue.

My grandfather studied maps
of stars and taught my mother
to connect the dots like making soup:
  potato
  carrot
  broth
but he never learned to say (I love you).

My grandfather sits sheathed and lidded
at one end of the table and my mother
tilts away from him like a roof of stars
headed for the other side of the globe

and I think we are always making wars
(my grandfather points jaggedly at the air)
and my mother's fingers cover
her eyes like constellations,
like pictures drawn across the sky.

The Navigator's Triangle

The stars were so many there, they seemed to overlap.
—Natalie Merchant

    Our necks should be built for looking upward,
    so we could stand for many hours
    next to each other, staring into the sky,
    and the weight of our eyes would not tilt
    onto our spines and remind us
    to look ahead, or down at the bones of our feet.

    Fifty years ago, my grandfather knew these stars
    like the streetlights in his own hometown:
    Ursa Major to Ursa Minor was like a walk
    around the block, to the North Star—a drive
    to my mother's school. He could take
    my mother outside, tilt her head up, and say
    this is the map of your world.
    But he couldn't say
    I know this because of the War.

    My mother has always said
    your grandfather doesn't talk about it.
    Doesn't talk about the years in planes
    with compasses, maps, and soldiers—
    how he guided them across the sky
    from the Navigator's Triangle outward—
    from Vega to the Northern Cross to Cassiopeia
    and told them just where to let it drop.

Last week I asked my grandfather if he knew
which planet hung in the sky across from us—
a lit face. He couldn't remember. Didn't know
that it was Jupiter, his moons circling
about him, all women: Leda, Io, Europa.
I stood next to my grandfather, looking
upward, my mother watching us from inside,
standing still as a point of light.

My mother does not know her father, and I
do not know what my grandfather knows—if
there are stars behind his eyes that no longer mean
what they used to mean, mapping a way
to people. Tonight the sky is dusted with stars
in patches dense as the track an eraser leaves
across a blackboard. Scorpius curls its tail
around Jupiter, the sign of my birth. And I imagine
my grandfather standing under this sky alone:
his head rocked back onto his spine like a fallen star,
his hands opening into emptiness, looking up.

In Tunnels Full of Wings

For sensible, wary miners, the bird goes first.
The small yellow head, feathers shivered
out like dandelion seeds, wings shocked
to spreading with the sudden chill—the surprise
of wind escaping earth to sky—the high,
lit song suddenly forgotten. Its eyes open
into tunnels, looking, looking, finding
nothing to reflect themselves upon.
It cannot even see its own body, everything—
feathers, wings, flight—slicked dark as coal.

My great-grandfather had no bird, but still
he was measuring breath. His wife, daughter,
son, living in the back of a butcher shop
in Benld, Illinois, the house front hung with meats,
facing Sixth Street in an offering of wings and limbs—
my great-grandmother carrying coal up from the basement
to heat the house from the back forward.

It was only once he was convinced to hide the shipment of sugar,
fresh off the river from St. Louis, deep in the mines—
coal carts heavy and still around him, the caves
as dangerous as the days of speakeasys, caution, flight.
Only once did he risk his family to have his turn
with them: *this time the favor falls to you, Anton Grosso.*
Nights long and suspended as the animals
hanging in the storefront—eyeless, mouthless, unable to run.
In one fist he holds the hand of my great-grandmother,
in the other the spreading fingers of my grandmother,
my great-uncle looking, looking, his eyes alert
in the dark place between then and now.

My great-grandmother, Celestina, died before
I was even conceived, and my grandmother suddenly
spread the sky before her. What was past
was gone: all the cleaving, all the coal dropped
down some dark shaft, a clattering of canary bones.
Her brother knows the stories, remembers more,
wears his name like a head of bright feathers.
He can see in the dark. He could hold a lantern in each hand.

My parents took my sister and me, as children,
to Georgetown, Colorado, to ride the open-carred train
through mountains holed out with gold mines.
I wanted to go inside one cave, to pass
into the borderland between light and discovery.
But with every step someone called out to me
Don't go in, don't go in. It could collapse at any time.
And what of my wings, opening into this tunnel
until I cannot see my cold breath circling at their tips?

Grandmother's Italian

Her head was filled with it—soft
as warm bread—
and she kneaded it between
her child lips as she stepped
into this country
in the American noise of 1923.

She grew to make our syllables
like sucking on cloves,
letting the lovely i's
fall away into the newspaper
headlines of crash and war.

Then, the size of sample shoes was 4 1/2,
which she wore like her native tongue.
Discounted for their smallness, these she carried
home with her eyes to the ground.

My grandfather was a navigator in the War.
His compass needled to
her diminishing Italian,
her empty purse, her tiny feet.

She spilled rolling s's on her wedding night
    fortissimo   *bellissimo*
until he trained her to his Tennessee accent.

Years of marriage like rows of spices,
rows of slender shoes—
her letters ground like peppercorns
into perfect syllables of sound.

Now, he corrects her perfect pronunciation
of the Italian dishes he cooks,
agreeing to his own Southern letters.
 oregano   olivo   amore
Her syllables fall silent, her feet
sit like spice jars, racked.

And I see that she remembers…
tasting phrases on her tongue…
but she has resigned herself
to the crumbling of *páne*.

The Engine

The Volkswagon's hollow backside
opens its empty mouth out
at us, cradling its 200-pound
engine between us, teetering
on 2x4's and a scissor jack
like a young bird stranded
at the edge of its nest.

It is so much for such
a small space, and our blackened
hands work it free of its steel body,
sighing into our arms with the weight
of a promise. My fingertips
drip oil and I think of my grandfather
in Colorado, his work in the oil industry.

All I know of oil is the lonely
pumping rigs I've seen
on the Texas landscape my family
drove through yearly in a Datsun
when I was young.
They rock like dinosaurs,
too obscene for the countryside—
having nothing of the dignity of windmills.

The engine pulls at the tendons
of my arms, and I look across to him—
whose eyes, whose touch, hold
me daily—whose arms nest me
nightly, whose presence makes me forget
this family I do not know.

My grandfather, stranger at the top
of the family tree, rocks there
conspicuous as an oil rig—while I learn
about mechanics here, 1200 miles
from my childhood home, from a car
as old as me and a pair of hands whose lines,
like my own, show clear and definite
as map lines through the thick oil.

The Volkswagon's shell yawns
out at us, the vacant shaft
missing the engine's bulk
the way I miss my grandfather
simply because he is old,
and I am related.

Remembering the weight in my hands,
I look across the engine at him,
lean into his lips
like a determined bird—
my young, new wings
struggling to hold up the sky.

For My Sister, Who Has Epilepsy

The voices you were hearing
when you were small, red-headed,
freckled like a pale sky
when the stars slip away
into the mouth of morning—
were real voices, knocking
at your eardrums like a filling
moon or a faint music box
or the soft fingering
of a branch on a window.

They were whispers from deep
within your skin, deep in your
hair, your heart, your eyes,
and you tried to listen
to them, tried so hard you
almost forgot, as you grew, the sound
of your own voice. But the language
was foreign, the words all wrong,
and you thought you might be one
of those mad women who
scrape themselves with their own
fingernails, count their freckles
unceasingly, or stare into the air
at nothing but the voices inside their heads.

When the twitching took you,
great shuddering of limbs,
in the long red-haired world
of your womanhood,
the voices were screaming and sobbing,
burrowing and shaking
themselves out of your skin,
your folded tongue,
the rolling whites of your eyes.

When you were small, and choking
on a piece of orange
while our mother worked
at your belly like a piston,
fisted your back in calm
terror—I stood and watched,
my hands at my throat, imagining
a scrap of orange meat there until
the one in your throat was forced
onto the floor at my feet, your voice
falling out after it
in screams and sobs.

So when the twitching took you
in its seizure arms
I, who was far away, could
picture you there on the floor,
your boyfriend on the telephone
to the hospital and our mother
while you thrashed and vibrated
in your own private
earthquake: the voices
so loud, so confusing, or perhaps
all at once so clear and understood:
sirens, life-long prescriptions,
and the ensuing silence.

Good Road Woman
for Estrella

Remember the sky you were born under,
know each of the star's stories.
—Joy Harjo

My cousins are a journey of stars, taking my whole
lifetime to reach me. You are the newest, the constellation
that has not yet risen over my patch of the earth.
I can only imagine your eyes, how they must be
like stepping stones, how they will take you
into this world. I think of your two names—one given
at birth, the other a gift of native blood—and know
I will meet you sooner than I found all the others.

Your brothers are new to me as first snow, as present
as the blue light of winter when so many stars
are sleeping. This past summer, in unusual rain, when
the days were just beginning to shut their doors
for an eager dusk, I met them. I was carrying my sister's
flowers, lace spread out behind her and a new ring
on her hand. My hair was up. At first, I did not recognize
your father, his beard gone, his smile the turning
of a new moon. It had been ten years. Your oldest brother
wore the cresting of his thirteenth year with a length
of quiet. Your second brother learned to play spoons
that night in my home, the reunited family wandering
through my rooms with startled affection.

Your sister is the cousin I did not know I had
until she grew nearly as tall as me, though our footsteps
fell over and over in the same state. Now, two months

after meeting her, I can see her face exactly: twin suns
in her cheeks and something of kin in her eyes. I glimpsed
a strength like water—constant and quick with change.

Cousin, I want to welcome you into this family
as you were welcomed into your name of stars and journeys.
May your hair grow long and dark, the way I remember
your mother's, though she is distant to me as any planet
you can name. May your eyes show you the gift
of your world. May your blood recognize its many forms.
Good Road Woman, I am hoping you cannot help but rise
into this name. May our paths cross soon, and often.
May you greet this family like a river, reminding us
of everything we've ever claimed as source.

Fox Pieces, Orcas Island

It is the island rummage sale, in the rain.
Here, everyone has what is necessary

and little that is not. The tables are lined
with bones, chicken feet, skins,

a headdress dangling small vertebrae
and soft, striped feathers. We stand before

a box labeled *fox pieces*, talk ourselves
into lifting the cardboard lid. Scraps of fur,

red hairs bristling on squares of skin.
You say your adopted brother would like

to be here, gathering bones and teeth.
Where is he this time, drinking, brown skin

bruising into blue? His hands bent
the dreamcatchers over our bed, tied the antler

bead to my wrist. You never know how
to touch him, what will bring him home.

With my eyes, I talk to the box of skins,
will the fox to assemble and walk into the rain.

Funeral

the boy squirms
runs to the back of the room
will not say goodbye
other children quiet
your small daughter gone home
three siblings hang together
candelabrum
your casket open-doored
dreamcatcher on your chest
all of us doors
on your journey
grandmother, everyone her bird
takes children in her hands
fireflies
cheeks glowing grief
so many names to remember
each photo a story
each person a landscape
each touch a small ghost
walking through walls
your daughter will remember you
like winter
in her bones
unrelenting
our dreams tangle
filter into our days
this day a child
holding a fallen bird

Ceremony
for my brother-in-law, Mitchell

my niece spells waterfall
leaves out the vowels
goes back for them
spirit world is sunrise
driving to Canada
offering cedar
tobacco
fire circled in stones
turkey vultures rise
over reservation
purple vetch
mother who raised you
names it fetch
something came for you
no one saw it coming
I did not notice
how they dressed you
so I picture you in fire
your daughter holds
onto your twin
says
I have nothing to say to waterfalls
says
my daddy is the pink clouds
tells us
my daddy is dead
we wrap sage bundles
listen to songs
drumming helps you leave
your daughter sleeps
in your brother's arms

my husband dreams
you calling
like you did at one a.m.
last of your voice
reaching us in sleep
we hold kittens at the farm
my niece brings them
to my lap all at once
three across in her arms
this child
your daughter
holds you
as the smoke of you
rises in her eyes

Crow Visitors

for my brother-in-law, Michael

On the first anniversary of your death,
I expect a crow to find me. I am here
at the Pacific's edge, tucked
between a patch of tall daisies and gray
crests of water returning, again and again.
I expect black wings to scatter the ghost
wisps of clouds, but there is only
the chaos of gull voices, and one
brown pelican after another.

Living, you walked that wavering
space between worlds, the one crows
warn us not to cross. On this side, you
amazed us with your kindness, your calm
way with our children, the work of your
large, brown hands. But the other
side always beckoned—you leaned
into the pull, accepting it would take
you young. You tilted drunkenly
toward that call when this earth-life
knocked you out cold, foul-breathed,
the needle still sunk in your arm.

The afternoon of your death, a crow
smacked into the window of our house
where I played with my children.
When we looked out the vibrating glass,
the bird had vanished—not teetering stunned
on the porch below, not flying into the blue
June day—just gone. Only later, when
I learned the time of your passing, was I
certain it was you, come to say goodbye.
The exact moment. That messenger crow.

When my small daughter sees a field
of crows laid out before her, she runs
to them, arms open, calling to them,
Chicken! Chicken! She is ecstatic, but
little legs disappoint her; the crows lift
and make for the light of the summer sky
before she has a chance to know them,
to remember the dark stars of their eyes.

But crows send her older brother panicking,
as if he thinks they will carry him off
like some shiny, enticing thing. In
a parking garage stairwell, trapped,
a crow whirrs about our heads. My son
screams like the very dead are after him,
though he understands little of death.
He is old enough to remember.

So I search for a sign that you
are safe now, somewhere trouble
cannot find you—perhaps a crow perched
next to its twin, your also-dead brother,
both of you who left us too soon
watching over our house this bright
day. With some measure of relief
in your crossing, in our grief we
miss the shape of you, the wide
laughter, the children in your arms. Tell
me that now you are not torn between
two worlds, now you have gathered
the glinting curio of this earth-life
and carried it back home.

Birds of Passage

i.

you tell me there's a stunned bird
on the sidewalk by the high rise
people stepping aside
as if it is nothing
but a lost tourist
you are on the 18th floor
maybe thinking
of the brother you lost
how he visits
your sister's rooms
his voice on the wind
you don't know
what kind of bird
some sort of hawk
don't know
if it flew into a window
fell many stories
is this how we are
with our grief
not knowing
building from sky
the police have closed
a lane of traffic
enough before rush hour
that it doesn't make
the news
we hope the phone
will never ring again
to tell us anyone we love
has died
by the end of the day

the bird is gone
and I want to know
where they've taken it
if wherever it is
will ever be safe enough

ii.

several states away
the smoke of your brother
pauses in the air
another hawk flattens
against a window
it is the house next door
to your brother's birthplace
no barriers
only reservation stillness
so much sky to choose from
who is he looking for
forgetting how to pass
through walls
we open and close our palms
blow out candles
burn sage
in the corners of rooms
the sky must be falling
stars smack into our windows
storm clouds spill under
our doors and the birds
double back on the wind
flying feet-forward
to land on our shoulders
whisper into our days
  we want to tell you something
  but we keep losing our way

iii.

four months to the day
and another
relative dies
we expect a hawk
to land on the windowsill
knocking
it is said
that when someone
we love has died
in twelve days
will come a sign
of safe passage
now all of us are looking
out our windows
through our dreams
into faces of people
we walk past
waiting for the message
hoping they will step
out of a crowd
calling our names

Sighting the Land

*Where we live in the world
is never one place.*

NAOMI SHIHAB NYE

Imagining Loons

My mother tells me I used to rub my chin
with tiny wet fists when I was a baby, and every
photo of me shows it's true—the space below my mouth
reddened as if with berry juice—as my fingers were
last weekend picking boysenberries in Oregon fields,
peach orchards bowing low to let us pass. Growing
up in Colorado, we had a cherry tree in the backyard—
a small one, enough for two cobblers every summer. Birds
dipped into the tree, wanting the cherries one at a time,
and we chased them off to gather handfuls, fill bowls.

But I was not born in the wide lap of plains stretching out
from the Rockies and their snowy heads. I was born in October,
when the aspen trees fill their hands with fool's gold,
inviting the wind to sing in small rustles or long, glittering
crescendoes of yellow. Three summers ago, driving
cross-country, Minnesota met me with a sudden embrace
of fog, took me aside and off the road, my first time back
since I was two years old. It was dawn. I was looking forward
to sunrise. Instead, we slept, waking into calm light, the last
of the fog lifting into rain. I wanted to drive to St. Louis Park, find
the hospital where I was born, but we pressed on, already late
and the lakes of Michigan waiting for us with still, blue patience.

So I have never heard a loon. Although my mother tells me
there were many near my grandparents' house, and they must
have sung me lullabies, coaxing my small fists into gentle, sleeping
palms. They must have heard me crying, their dark heads tilting
at the sound. But I cannot remember the trees, the snow, the water,
or their voices welcoming me into the world. In Colorado, I loved
magpies and swallows, birds with distinctive shape to their tails
and wings. In Oregon, my mouth drops slightly open at the sight
of herons, their slow, blue forms reminding me of that morning sky
in Minnesota, my hand cupped over my lips and chin in quiet,
   startled awe.

But it was the loons who sang to me before the aspens,
whose voices lifted my eyes into woods—my little hands
struggling with the weight of my head—long before the mountains
showed me where the sky ends. How could I have forgotten?
It is almost autumn here in Oregon. The berries are falling
from the vines. Soon everything will be as red—flares
of yellow and orange crowding out the green. But I am imagining
the dark shapes of loons I have never seen, their fine, slick bodies
on the water, their long mouths opening slightly
into a deep, patient summoning home.

Denver's Rain

The gutter in front of our house on Glencoe Street
had a section wide and deep as the bowl
of a pelvis, rimmed with asphalt that softened
with the heat, fingered into the cracks
of the concrete, steamed and hissed
when the rains began. Late summer
afternoons in Denver meant thunderstorms,
the sky opening up and the full gong
of the storm resounding in my five-year old body.

Severe Thunderstorm Watch—it was still safe
to be playing outside with my sister, the hose
spreading sheets of water down the driveway
and into the Big Gutter. My mother was still
snapping beans on the front porch, silver
mixing bowls at her browned bare feet. We
could hear the wind leaning into the crabapple tree
in the backyard with its moist breath
of thunder, the tree rocking in and out
of the dark sky and dropping its red fruit.

Severe Thunderstorm Warning—we had to pull
everything in—shut off the hose as the sky,
cracking, let the first drops fall. We gathered
up our cats as our mother collected her beans
and moved us into the house. The small
TV brightened before us and we watched the weathermen
on Storm Center 4 point out tornadoes, fascinated, secretly
hoping one would head for our house.

My mother tried to keep us away from the windows,
but we wanted to watch the lightning, count
the storm's movement towards us in the seconds
between the split and the sky rolling itself
whole again—wanted to watch the Big Gutter
fill until it spilled onto the sidewalk, the water
rushing around the block like our dog
when he got loose, hail the size of ping pong balls
casting the lawn into winter. And we sat
in the dark of the house, the crabapple tree
losing leaves a season too soon, thinking
of the possibilities of mud and bluing skies,
the gutter now indistinguishable from the body of the storm.

Leaving a House

I am surprised to be missing the way the dust
collected behind doors and on the leaves
of the ficus tree, the way the low breath
of last winter's wind spilled beneath the door
and followed me through rooms the way I followed
your trail of yesterday's shirts, notes,
plates of graham cracker crumbs, green olive oil.
I did not expect to miss the bathroom walls—
paint curling up like orange rind, rich
odor of mildew—or the dirty spot at the base
of the refrigerator, the creak of the bedroom floor.

Where I live now, I cannot hear the rain
on the roof or the pigeons cooing on weekend
mornings. I do not hear your breath beside
me, the shift of the bed frame as you turn
your back to me. There is a quiet space
around me like an empty cup, like wind
ceasing for one moment on a mountaintop.
I look at my hands over and over,
wondering where your hands have gone.

I remember the sound of the doorbell—
a child striking a pot with a wooden spoon—
remember how I opened up for you,
how I took you into my rooms, my arms,
my most private expectations. From our window
we could climb onto the roof—watch
the sunset and my cat chasing beetles
through the overgrown dandelions—where I climbed
the night you started sleeping in another room,
your footsteps turning to footprints
I followed through the house in circles,
again and again turning back upon myself.

Last week I went back for one last thing—you were
not home—and trespassed through rooms scattered
with disregard—coats, books, empty cups. The rhododendron
was blooming deep red, I brought in the mail
out of habit, I expected you around each corner.
Today I walk that house by heart—my passage
rehearsed with years. I want to take doors,
cabinets, windowsills—tuck them into
my pockets to draw out later when I am sitting
in a place I cannot call home—press them into the walls
the way my fingers used to press into your shoulders—
you rising above me like the landscape of home, our two
breaths the only sound in the house.

Landscape

I am leaving the only space I found
by myself—small apartment snuggled into
a Portland neighborhood of coffeeshops, bookstores,
and tall Victorian houses with their many windows,
dormers, widow's walks looking out onto bridges
and lights instead of empty seas. The small apartment
whose windows face east onto a garden I have watched
be planted, turned, and replanted. The school
bus stop where I have watched the children
spread and cluster in the mornings, gathering
their thirteen years around them like mounding seeds.

I remember my mother pushing seeds into small hills
of dirt in our Colorado garden to grow squash,
zucchini, pumpkins. How she planted marigolds at the edges,
pulled carrots, snapped beans, pinched tomato hornworms
in half with her one-fingered trowel—their green, knobbed bodies
arching back into the soil on either side—my sister and I looking
over her shoulder with twisted mouths. How before the garden
there was only sloped, dry dirt, tumbleweeds stumbling
their way down the street lined with no houses,
then our house, then the house across the street,
then the whole suburban pattern of houses
darkening the sky, the tumbleweeds vanishing
like stars into the rising light of day.

My sister and I saved the tumbleweeds for as long
as we could, piled them up in a corner of the backyard,
until the snow came and found them huddled
there together, curling into each other the way a baby
holds on to a thumb. When April turned the last
of the snow back to water again, they were a mass
of wet sticks, a flattened nest, mulch for my mother's

garden. When July came with its hands
of afternoon thunder, its tornado breath, I had already
begun to forget.

I am only now remembering tumbleweeds,
black-eyed thunderstorms, rain that bears
weight. Remembering snow up to my knees,
hail the size of worry stones, always knowing
which way was west by where the mountains
framed the world. Only now remembering
in this city where the volcano only sometimes
shows its face, where the rivers run with salmon
instead of gold, where I am closer to the place
where the women watched from their balconies
for anything to crest the horizon of the sea.

And I stand quietly in this window
before leaving: watch for something to point
its way toward me and call it home.

Letter in a Flood
for Portland

City, I have been trying to tell you something for many weeks. But you keep changing the weather. The first time, I wanted to show you how the space between my two nipples, the space I cannot quite touch by dipping my chin, has filled up with something I found all over again, like the broken-winged pigeon I buried in the pansy garden where I later tried to plant wildflowers. And you sent wind, making the trees drop their arms for you, building small gates across your streets so you could spend one night alone. The next time, I wanted to take off my socks and stretch out my toes to you, fanning into new places I'd been. You brought me ice instead of rain, and everything lay still, expectant. Then I wanted to sing you something and you filled my mouth with snow. I tried to be angry, but you were too quiet and turned yourself sunlit and blue, reminding me of home, how this day was not yours, but something you had borrowed for me from halfway across the country, trying to make me homesick, to keep me from loving you so much I couldn't leave. And today, I tell you I might go for just a little while, I promise to come back, I say you like my own name, I talk to you like you are listening. And city, today you have sent this flood, this real flood that fills newscasts and tumbles houses and drives rats into the daylight. Your river rises to embrace its bridges, you close my favorite drawbridge down, its arms thrust into the warm, wet air like two great firs. And it is all happening slowly: you sound like a soft storm in off the coast, you inch your way up the seawall. And city, I understand. You are overflowing, you are washing yourself for the first time in many years, you are ecstatic with rain, you are taking it all back. So how could I ever go?

Visiting Lighthouses

You and I have been married one week, and now
on the Three Capes Loop of the Oregon coast
what is important is calla lilies, herons at dusk
with their feet in low tide. The days are landscaped
with breakfasts, afternoons of sun and my hair
tied up, harbor seals eyeing us at Strawberry Hill.
We climb the twist of steps in the lighthouse
at Cape Meares, look at one another through opposite
sides of the original lens, now still and unlit, removed
from the memory of ships. At Heceta Head, we walk
past the haunted keeper's house and up the hill
to where the lighthouse, its windows bricked in,
still blinks its pattern of flashes, a conversation of comfort
by which ship captains navigate their way around land.
We hear stories, lenses shipped here in molasses to keep
them whole, thrown overboard, buoyed to shore, unpacked
and polished until they lost their hoods of thick liquid,
arriving transparent at the lighthouse tower.
We are told how the keeper used to strain the kerosene
through silk so the lenses would not blacken as the light
burned. I watch you across the small room beneath
the active lens, think of the keeper welcoming the company
of ghosts, someone with whom to share this view of sky
and the white lines of waves gathering toward shore.

Nests

I am one week into living in this new city, set among Oregon's hills and the quiet darkness of woods. Deer have visited us, I am hearing crickets again, the stars here seem close and numerous enough to run my hands through. In Colorado, my mother's husband has cleaned out the garage and discovered a box I hid there as a girl, pigtailed tomboy keeping to myself. He sends it to me. It arrives today, and I pull open the flaps of the box, marked in my childish hand, *Nature's Artifacts. Handle with care. Do not throw away.* It is a quiet morning, and I am taken back to skinned knees and hole-worn Keds as I lift birds' nests, petrified wood, river rocks and pinecones, pussy willows, a cocoon, the half-decayed remains of snakes. I line them up across the kitchen counter and remember trips to the mountains, the color of aspen in autumn. Here, my cat brings a garter snake into the house, and I see my ringless, girl hands as I pick it up, pinching it behind the head, to take it back outside. Last night, an animal fell into our chimney, scattered soot as it tried to scale the walls to escape. This morning all is still, and I think of settling in to this city where I know no one, shifting birds' nests in my hands—feathers, grass, mud, all woven into a bowl—a home that I found and kept, and now has returned to me.

Birdwatching

Anniversary, we drive to the herbary
on the island—sun visiting for the first time
in days, stretches of orchards, ripening
berries. We buy stevia for the sweetness, strong
oregano, soft shoots of lamb's ear. An oriole, yellow-
feathered, distinct, comes to the hummingbird
feeder—nothing in us wants to leave.
Before moving back to this city we missed,
a man measured barometric pressure
by the height swallows fly—the higher
the pressure, the higher the insects—the lower
the pressure, the more dipping low of the birds,
predicting the weather, when the rains will come.
In the city we left, quiet with deer and hills,
I watched every small thing—waited daily
for ducklings when the brown mother duck
disappeared to nest. Nothing here is familiar,
everything is more difficult than I thought.
Naturalists on television are walking on obsidian,
negotiating the glass of the lava flow with careful steps.
The ground beneath them is shattering—the sound
is wings beating earth instead of air.

Islands

My windowsill is lined with memories the size of pockets,
the weight of lifting in palms, the color of being noticed,
being kept. These stones have been gathered from coastlines,
sent from hometowns, brought back by friends visiting
other time zones. They form a small line of looking outward,
slipping into color as the morning comes into light.
Today I look out onto heavy rain, gray skies, a wish
to visit someplace else—to move, for awhile, to more rain
but green hills, sea birds, the smell of wool.

I have heard that the land in Ireland is parceled by rock
walls, stands of crumbling stone where once there were no gates,
wood too precious for the likes of passage. I imagine patient
sheep, water balling on their thick coats while they wait
as the wall is disassembled each morning for them to walk
through, built up again each evening to keep them home.
The repeated lifting of stones, the intimacy that must have come
to burden each one in the quiet of dawn and dusk.

I lift a rock from Orcas Island off the sill—its smooth, dark shape
marbled with white lines, mapping rivers that match
the texture of my palms. I recall standing in a stone tower
overlooking what should have been the San Juans—but instead
was clouds, the illusion of trapped space. I landed the last step
down from the tower, thinking what the view might have been,
when the clouds pulled back, the shape of islands appearing
full circle as I turned. And this was not confinement,
but where one would go to test the unfolding of wings.

This is why sheep stand in the rain. They are not stranded, knowing as we sleep, we count them jumping. It is enough like flying. This is how I know it is time to go. And why long for an island, a ship of landscape anchored by sea on all sides? Why long for cliff sides, sea birds rising and dipping in the wind? Why long to lay hands upon those gateless rock walls, but for the knowing that each stone is a possible door— that every direction I turn, there is only sky.

Driving to the San Juans

We wonder if we'll hit rush hour
north of Seattle, into Everett,
not reach the exit for Mt. Vernon
until the sun drops
behind the Sound.
The long road to the ferry
will be dark, fields on either side
vanishing into dusk, the water tower
tall and shadowed, hardly a landmark.
When the radio turns to static
we'll listen to the road opening.
Everything in the car will settle
into stillness—the suitcases,
uneaten sandwich halves,
books we might not have time to read,
maps of the island we are already
memorizing with our visits.
Have we always been this quiet
with each other? I can't think
of one thing to say. I will watch
your knuckles on the wheel, the light
of your eyes as we pass the reservation.
Then Anacortes, and we'll turn
down the sleepy streets,
racing the ferry. We'll follow
signs printed with boats, arrows,
coast down the winding hill.
The ferry will rise to meet us, lit
and rimmed with green. And we'll travel
from one island to another, the ground
rising out of the water, wind pushing
cormorants and gulls. And you will lean
into me, settling into stillness. Were we ever
headed anywhere else?

Construction
Eastsound, WA

From Prune Alley step across back door
into market, through. Under the street
human dinosaurs—the county is laying pipe
beside them, not telling anyone—leaving them.
Who would know—Main Street—monkey puzzle
trees keeping watch? New benches for greenspace
near the library—underneath?—lava flow,
hardened, whole island of earthquakes.
Mr. Lavender's chickens near the fence—we walk past.
Feathers are sunrises, wings are sky. Behind church,
wind off the Sound, in front orange cones
are any other detour—not bodies. Not these—
bones of quiet here before the town, before
the market backed up against Prune Alley, before chickens
forgot about wings. Sleep of islands, camera of deer.
In the street, a whole new noise gathers.

This Anniversary, I Am in San Francisco

My friend was right, today there is wind—
cool air moving my shoulders to shudder a little.

The bridge is long and disappears into the city.
A cluster of harbored sailboats, sails drawn in,

display their masts like winter trees. Stone benches
warm in the sun. A small child on a bicycle tests

his training wheels, his father following behind.
He vrooms in Spanish. My own city is smaller

than this. Today, my husband and I have known
each other seven years. He is a voice on the telephone,

surrounded by rain. Ice plants turn pink offerings
from the hills. Landing, I could see them

from the plane. The bay is quiet with sailboats.
Ferries change places like gulls. Mid-afternoon.

The clock chimes from the edge of the water.

Wind River

From the riverbed, we watch satellites
   small lights traveling in arcs
      lights fall into the curve
         of Earth—

We are left in this hemisphere
   tilted toward the sky
      holding our bodies with both hands
         both hands reaching—

Bears hibernate—sleep curled into themselves
   months and months pass
      bears sleep—their muscles do not change.
         When they wake up, they walk away.

We watch satellites, feel ourselves falling
   ease our bodies into steaming springs
      naked
         hold our bodies with both hands—

Astronauts look out small windows at Earth
   press their hands, fingers wide, against the glass
      months and months pass.
         Home, if they try to walk away, their leg bones shatter.

River falls into the curve of Earth
   months and months pass—we hold our bodies
      with both hands, naked
         our hands make arcs, reaching —

Scientists try to keep muscle strong to bone
   keep bones from shattering
      when we step into the world.
         We look out small windows. We watch the sky.

Architecture

On an afternoon in Annisquam, Massachusetts,
when I was young and she was younger,
a child showed me how to scoop a handful
of wet sand, close a fist around its soft weight,
and let it fall in a slim stream to form castles
whose towers rose in lumps and swirls, an impossible
balancing. She called this *dribbling*, a technique
with no pail-shaped mounds, no smoothed sides,
no moats. Every sandcastle I'd ever made was suddenly
flattened, taken back to sea. At the tip
of this stretch of beach is a lighthouse, and behind
it the path to Squam Rock—a boulder so large and round
you could climb it only from one angle, with a running start,
and watch the ocean appear where a moment ago
there was only beach grass and sky. Later, visiting
Annisquam's town hall, I would stand on a twist of stairs
to read the names of sailors lost at sea—their fine, New England
names stacked on the wall in a layering of paint and brick
as if their memories alone kept the building rigid and whole.
And I would visit cemeteries, stones chipped and worn almost
too smooth to decipher, entire plots hidden in the woods
of someone's backyard. I would take pictures, balancing
the lens in an air rich with cricket noise and salt.
And before leaving, the ribbon for a new bridge would
be cut by a woman 107 years old, her wheelchair guided
by a seven year-old girl—the ribbon falling on either side
so that we all might travel and return.

Housewarming

I have a friend who doesn't like houses. She calls
them boxes, feels trapped inside. Even if the doors
are open and the windows have no screens, and no matter
the size or number of rooms, she can't relax under
a roof. Ancient rhetoricians believed in the power of roofs—
they were necessary to keep conversations from being lost
to the skies. I believe in the power of doorways—
of thresholds, exits, entryways, and crossings.

Though I found a place to live two weeks ago, I am still
reading the classifieds: Three bedrooms. Hardwood floors.
                  Studio. Near bus line. Victorian triplex.
                  W/D hookups. No pets no pets no pets.
                  Open Sunday 10-2.
I want to visit them.
I want to peek into all of the rooms, open closets and cabinets,
test faucets, look into and out of the windows. Ring
the doorbell. Flush the toilet. Check if the sills
are wide enough for cats. I want to imagine where
I would put the couches, what could grow in the yard. I think
who might have lived there, who could live there next.

The street I am moving to has no name, but a number. I'm used
to that; I've had a post office box for eight months. I'm going
to move out of this box into porch swing, fireplace,
claw foot bathtub, gas stove. I will plant peas, basil, cilantro.
My cats will move freely in and out. I will dust mop
the hardwood floors, make sun tea, walk up and down
the stairs. I will have conversations with the walls
and they will remember. I will stand on both sides
of the doorways and feel safe either way. I will do
what children do with boxes: fill them with the best things,
the biggest secrets—and lift the lid as often as I want.
My own cupboards will surprise me. I will invite my friend
over and she will make herself at home. She will feel
exactly as she does when standing in the sun.

Uncharted Worlds

I would know this world anywhere
as my son's world, I would love it any time in his name.

SHARON OLDS

The Day After Finding Out My Sister is Pregnant

My sister lives on an island—ferries press in
and out again; deer live there. To see a slim doe
cross the winding road lined with wind sculptures,
where everyone waves in passing, it is a wonder
how this animal came here at all. So much water,
they must have flown here like scattered seeds.
On this island, there are many potters, so the days
are filled with shaping wet clay and warming kilns
for firing. The post office is a world all its own.
Everywhere letters come from is far away.
I think of the shop I pass on my way to work, a sign
out front tempting *Angels Sold Here*.
It is as incredible as deer on an island, as voices
traveling through telephone wires, as the way
she caught this week's full moon to keep inside
of her until it warms to shining.

At Six Months

We are in the channel, rounding the fingers
of Sucia Island, looking for a place to pull in.

Three bald eagles lift from the rocks
as our boat spins by, slows to watch them.

Today, we have been watched by harbor seals,
eyeing my sister's belly—round as their own.

I imagine Irish fishermen, telling their children
how those large wet eyes were part human,

seal people who could slip from their skins on land.
My sister's bellybutton is disappearing, her skin

stretches and grows taut, smooth. Her hands rest there
like nested birds, rise to push her hair from her eyes.

I move my hand to feel the kicking, but all
is still. Soon, this roundness will fall away,

she will wear skin slightly large, newly drawn on.
Near midnight, we see flashes of light

from the porch, drive to the water's edge to watch
the sky. But it is a false alarm of northern lights—

only heat lightning reaching into the Sound.
The sky is restless and ablaze.

Messengers
for Grayson Wolf

    i.

Today, you are born where ravens talk with the voices
of people, where deer swim from island to island, naming
them *first home* and *next home* and *next*. You will journey
by water and your eyes will open onto birds: eagle,
cormorant, kingfisher, towhee. I know a woodpecker
lives near your bedroom window, a screech owl
in your backyard. They will invent your lullabies. You
will sleep as they shed rain from their wings. Today,
the moon is full. Your new body is welcomed by light.
Already, you are eager for your name.

    ii.

It is a week since your birth, and today a pod of orcas
is sighted off the coast of Seattle, moving south.
I think they are messengers from your home headed
toward mine. They tell me your eyes are two blue
stones from where your island eases into the Sound.
Your skin, soft as Madrone bark, remembers
the earth. Here, I find my eyes fill with water
at every gentle thing. Through the phone, I hear
you crying. You must be talking to the birds.
I imagine your tiny hands opening, sending them on.

iii.

The morning I am leaving the island after meeting
you, three birds assemble outside my window
in Massacre Bay. They wait for me to walk
down weathered stairs to the pebbled shoreline,
long cormorant neck and restless gull eyes small
against the blue length of heron. By the time
I drive away, there is only the tall bird left. Later,
when I develop the pictures I took, you are smiling
with your eyes closed. At one month old, the tide
has moved full cycle. Everything it brings
                                                it brings again.

Everything

    Buh Buh Buh
       means everything
the dog scratching at the door for dinner
      and you small, your sight grows longer
          longer with each day
      your fingers learn to hold on to everything
      everything has a taste
the dog scratching at the door for dinner
      you want to be there when he is fed
         feel his fur
         in your fingers
         learn to hold on to everything
when the woman who carries you
    steps out to feed the dog
the dog scratching at the door for dinner
      you say Buh Buh Buh
         mean everything
         want to be outside with the dog
         with the red hair of the woman
         with the dog eating his dinner
         everything has a taste
you say Buh Buh Buh
     three teeth coming in, your teeth come in
        more with each day
    your fingers learn to hold on to everything
you say Buh Buh Buh
    and mean the dog, mean where you want to be
outside the door
the woman with the red hair who carries you
holds everything

Weather Conditions

O'Hare Airport. The screen at the gate announces
the weather in Portland, Oregon. Not partly cloudy,
not rain, not chance of thunderstorms, but these:
towering cumulus clouds.
It is almost a poem, or a prophecy crafted by an oracle
for the women weeping at her feet—
please promise us crops. Sun. Rain. But
not these, not towering cumulus clouds—
somehow sentient, and foreboding, a knock at the door
long into night that sets the dog to barking. Cats
spring from the bed, and you sit upward from a dream
without clouds. You can remember nothing.
You touch your belly—something is building there, too—
it lengthens, shifts, and you have been waiting in
concentration to feel it moving—more like moonlight,
a shaft of sun through trees—not towering
cumulus clouds—which are what, exactly?
What will meet you when you step off the plane?
Your husband waiting, how he'll touch
the nape of your neck, drive you home.
Will the rains have come by then, or passed,
while you have been flying through sky, wind, maybe rain,
maybe towering cumulus clouds. Will the rains have
come? Will the sky be open and new?

Three Days

The repetition of division, small firefly
of heartbeat, buds of arms and legs, soft
ladder of spine. Eyes that find comfort
in darkness. Ears that remember heartbeat,
voice. Pulse of cord that sustains one life
with another, breath passing in a whisper
of blood, the bodies telling secrets to each
other: muscle, skin, bone.

A string of miracles so precise
and improbable, even a non-believer
might be tempted to consider God.
So who are we to ask for yet another
miracle? But we do. We wish
for *perfect*, and *healthy*. And then still
for *handsome*, and *intelligent*, and *kind*.

When I am two months pregnant,
I hear of a baby girl born missing
a section of her heart. She defies
statistics and lives. Strong. Fragile.
Beautiful. No one would have given her back.

So when my son is born and will not nurse,
cannot get enough breath into his perfect, new
lungs, my body will not consider anything
but healing. He has inhaled amniotic fluid,
perhaps unwilling to leave his first home behind.

For three days we live as two separate beings.

Oxygen hoods. IVs. Clear, insubstantial
tubes mocking my body's ability to keep
him whole. But after the first hours, he nurses,
and then he will not let go. After three days
of doctors, nurses, and a long hallway between
us, he comes home. I carry him everywhere.

I try to erase those three days. That's not how
we started, is it, little one? We started skin
to skin, fluid to fluid, hand to hand. Mouth
to nipple. Eye to eye. Heartbeat to heartbeat.
We started when I first felt you flutter
inside me. And before that, when I first
imagined you there. And you were there.

Yoga as a Mother

For the duration of my hour
and a half yoga class, children
are playing loudly on the street outside.

Though I don't need a reminder
to think of my son. Even when I am
not with him, I can feel him in my body.

It is impossible to clear my mind in meditation.
Impossible to be the corpse that is shavasana. I am
always aware of his small hands, his loud voice.

My lower back, slightly sore
from lifting and carrying his twenty
pound, wriggling body.

My arms, stronger now in warrior
after holding him for ten months.
Stronger legs holding horse stance.

My breasts, full of milk because
it has been two hours since he nursed.
I cannot rise into cobra without noticing.

My belly, trimmed with extra skin,
my core not as strong as before
his small life grew inside me.

When my limbs shake holding plank,
when I am taking Ujjayi breaths in downward
dog, I am thinking of 21 hours of labor.

No asana will ever be as long, or as
difficult. Thinking of his birth
puts all effort into perspective.

If I could birth this child without drugs,
with such focus, without sleep, then surely
I can hold chaturanga one more breath.

If I can love someone this much, this
fiercely, then surely I can let each thought
go and clear this mind. Kapalabhati.

Breath of fire. *Skull shining.*
Like my son's head emerging in such
heat. I will never be able

to be empty.

Faith as a Mother

I am listening to the woman
being interviewed on the radio.
Her son has been killed in Iraq.

She has another son who says
he would still go, if called. When
the interview begins, I expect

hysteria. A choked voice. At least
tears. But she is entirely calm. She says
I am completely at peace.

*God has a plan. It may be different
than my plan. But he has a plan.*
I am in awe of such faith.

Since my son was born, I cannot
imagine anything more immense
than my love for him. Anything

more terrible than him being taken
from me. If there is a god who can
overpower such love—

I never want to meet him.

Small Talk

I've been thinking of it
as the "poetry party", this night
out to celebrate a friend's
book publication. I don't
get out much anymore. I've written
only three poems since the birth
of my two-year old son.

All the city's literati
are here. I know some, get
introduced to others. I'm not
good at small talk. For two
years, when someone asks,
so, what have you been doing?
I say, *my son really likes
things with wheels.*

Every poet-friend asks,
so, have you been writing?
It's impossible to give
a suitable explanation
to people without children,
to people who don't
know my child.

I have nothing to say
about my writing. And who
here would understand
about how all day I give
words to this child who
is late to talk? All day I take
indistinct syllables of sound
and give them meaning, weight.

I put consonants after vowels.
I add adjectives for encouragement.
I interpret. I do my best to guess.
I soothe scream after frustrated
scream. By day's end, I've used up
all my words. I've given them away.

So when the poet-friend asks
have you been writing? I am relieved
when her partner comes to my rescue,
says, *she has a young child and you
ask her that?* And laughs. Another
mother. One who raised a son
by herself. She says, *keep
a journal. Just write things down
when you can.*

I decide I will try to put some words
down, like hoarding pennies
in a jar. For later. For a rainy day.
For when my son can finally tell me
what he's thinking, what he wants.
For when every sentence is
miraculous. And everyone will be
listening.

Echolalia

My late-talking son is talking
all the time now, a nonstop flow of syllables
and phrases that come out the same every time.
Broken record doesn't even begin to tell the story.
My life with him is a soundtrack of repetition.

The word itself is lovely, echolalia,
and reminds me of bats. How they find insects
in the dark. And each other. Instinctual,
utterly important. Echolocation.
This is how I see my son's language.
He's finding us in the dark, he's showing us
where he is.

He offers phrases from his favorite books
as greeting, conversation.
On Thursday he ate through four strawberries.
A comb and a brush and a bowl full of mush.
And when he woke up, he found it was true.
And they went out together into the deep, deep snow.

And what if we all listened this intently?
What if we remembered what was said?
Repeated ourselves until we got a response?
Until we heard our own words
echoed back to us?

To fight discouragement, to tell myself that someday
he will say he loves me, to imagine the conversations
we will have, I try to think of his words as heartbeats.
A rhythm that is essential, utterly important.
The sound he is using to find his way out.
The sound that keeps us alive. The sound that ties me
to him, beat for beat, and word for word.

Sensory Profile

i

I could pretend I know
what you're thinking when
you're spinning wheels, your eyes
intent on the turning, your body
remarkably still. Or spinning
yourself, never dizzying, eyes
tuned to the whirl of the room. You
are running now, back and forth,
circling, colliding your quick
little body over and over into
my body, or any soft thing.

ii

The way you are immobilized
if I remove your shoes on the lawn.
How you hold out your hands
for me to brush off the sand, every grain
too overwhelming to touch.
How this food is not warm enough,
that one is too slimy, this one
is not a perfect rectangle. You melt
before my eyes. We rock and sing,
rock and sing, rock and sing.

iii

My driver's window opening is acceptable–
fresh air. Your back window opening
sends you panicking like a trapped bird.
Your eyes widen and tear, you try
to lean away in your car seat. You are quiet,
terrified, eye of a storm about to shift.
But then the streetlamps set your eyes
steady, focused. You center and lean
into their glow, their simple illumination
of what a moment ago we couldn't see,
what gradually moves into our view.

iv

How you love to cross bridges.
Vibration of the steel under the car, lights
in neat, bright lines, the river beneath
a soft rushing, the bridge lifting us
to safe architecture of air. You love
the ones with perfect angles and x's.
Those lit like a ladder of stars.
And the kind that were built improbably.
Lowered whole from the sky.

Hollows

The place in my body you used to be.
Now my heart is on the outside.

The quiet when you finally fall asleep
in my arms. If you are awake, you are crying.

The days, the months and months
of you not talking, your lack of words.

The silence after the meltdowns. We
wait out the calm for another storm.

The things you won't touch, won't
eat, won't tolerate, won't do. It is like

where we are when the birds
leave us in winter. But I remember

we planted things, we tended,
nurtured, nourished, and warmed.

The birds will come back to us.
All of this will bloom.

Signs

My three-year old can name
any sign on the road. He knows
the letters, shapes, symbols, colors.
If we are walking, he likes to touch
the weathered faces, wrap his fingers
around the posts, name and rename.

STOP
Some days, I feel sunk in cement.
I can't move my feet, can't see
past the rain in my eyes. The world
approaches, stares, leaves us behind.
We perseverate together—he recites
the letters again and again.
S. T. O. P. No instructions
for which way to turn.

YIELD
The road moves in to meet us. Hands
on the wheel, I resist taking my turn.
I'm afraid if we merge, we'll be stuck
in this traffic forever. We'll never
get home. Someone honks. I inch forward,
check the blind spots, shift gears.

NO U-TURN
We wouldn't go back even if we could.
We have navigated dodgy side streets,
gotten lost, asked for directions. Used
up a profusion of fuel. We've sat in
noisy intersections, wound down quiet
roads. He points ahead. *This way.*

ONE WAY
Forget about the map. We memorized
its lines, then left it at the rest stop
three states back. This is only one direction,
one arrow, and he wants to see
them all. Left turn, right turn, two-way
traffic, curve. We might go around the block.
We might drive for miles and miles.

BUMPS
We spend a lot of time with this sign.
It's one of his favorites–we see
it on our daily walk. We know
its shape, its angles, its warning face. But
the road between us and the playground
is in constant flux. Broken glass, a new
flower, bees. And always, he must
touch this sign before we can go home.

CONSTRUCTION AHEAD
We might be here awhile. Expect delays.
Or maybe it's Sunday and the workers
have the day off, the road signs are pushed
to the side. But we're curious. What
are they building? Does it have scaffolding,
are they tearing up the street? When
we round the next corner, will there be
a road block, a detour, a flagger waving
us through? I look back at him.
Green light. *Go.*

Dipper

It's not what you expect, this bird,
this Ouzel feathered
like any other bird, beaked
like any other, winged and
skin-footed and dark-eyed but
then it begins, the quick plié over
and over and then the diving,
yes, the swimming, it goes
under like a fish, emerges slick,
water beading, still a bird and
still singing, and
still able to fly.

So when my son stands out
from the others, not playing
tag, not swinging or sliding but
instead pretending to ride
an elevator, up and down, floor
to floor, making the sounds,
perfect mechanical tones,
a small, remarkable rush
of a boy, rough-haired and
torn-kneed as any other—well,
I think, he's just
the unexpected, just the thing
you think you know
but you don't.

What They Won't See

Finally, after unspectacular years in the windows
of our small string of homes, our night blooming cereus
is budding. A bud the size of an egg, wrapped in long,
purpled tendrils muzzling forward to the tip, perched
at the end of a thick, curving stalk. It is the last week
of June in a summer slow to arrive, cast in cloud cover
and rain after rain. We are tired—a week of children
coughing in their sleep, of night terrors and moving
from their beds into ours. But we will stay up to see it open,
perhaps tonight, perhaps tomorrow, watch the tendrils
peel back to reveal feathery white petals, a bird of a blossom
spreading its full, fragrant body forward into the dark.

We don't want to miss it. But also today, I am thinking
of what our dead are missing. What they won't see.
Their deaths are still close, near enough that our children
remember them with equal parts confusion and longing.
Sometimes I can accept that they are gone. But not the morning
we wake to find our son has grown taller overnight. Not the day
my husband arrives home from a long weekend trip to remark
that our daughter is bigger. Her body fills up more space,
her toes reach out farther into the room. Not the times
when these children unfurl with their growing, so quickly
you can almost see their young arms lengthening toward the sky.
And I think, how can they be sleeping, our dead? *Wake up.*
Be here to see this. You can't miss this flowering, this bloom.

Journeys & Returns

Try to be one of the people on whom nothing is lost!

HENRY JAMES

Wind Horses

In Bhutan, prayers are written on flags
lining monastery walls, words
offered into the skies and carried away.
Buddhists call these *wind horses*.
Here, whole land masses away, the air
is still and hot—even the voices of birds
do not reach far. I think of writing a letter,
small telling that will journey days and by then
the story will have changed. I may even forget
the order of my words, the specific phrasing.
By the time an answer comes, the Earth
may have tilted such that the weather is new,
a deep wind rises up, and even when I shout
it is difficult to know if I've been heard—
which direction these hopes have been carried.

Travel
a letter to Christine

This week began with Amelia Earhart, how I heard
another woman is beginning the same journey, following
the same path in the same kind of plane, though with
    instruments
updated for communication and navigation. She hopes
to make it across the Pacific, trusting her wings to lift her
where Amelia's failed, falling into the sea
for daring to stare into the sun. I can check her progress
hourly on the web, know when she is in New Orleans,
Venezuela, Senegal, Greece, Egypt, Indonesia, Hawaii. I dream
of traveling to Ireland, Italy—then wrap my arms more tightly
around home, think of more and more reasons to stay.

It also began with the cherry trees coming into bloom, except
this year it was still raining, the blossoms folding their wet faces,
thinking they had waited all this time for nothing. Last year,
the year before, the sun greeted them, framed them in blue,
caught their silken heads in an offering of light—as it does finally
today, at the end of the week, coaxing the champagne blooms
into warming March air. Soon there will be wind, scattering
the petals as they flutter, with reluctance, to earth.

I re-read your letter, think of how you spent Christmas—
alone in South America, quiet at Machu Picchu with its meander
of river, its three sides of mountains a kind of prayer. You write
to tell me how this place drew you, called you to a kind of home.
You tell me of the roofless structure with two bowls carved
into its floor, filling with rainwater to reflect the stars. There,
you were not thinking of the dogs who tore your pant leg
in Chile, the men who whistled at you in the dirty streets.
You might be thinking of the people who gave you food as you
    wandered
an unfamiliar city with nothing over your head but the sky—or

the geology you came here to study—the rocks telling you
 their stories,
introducing you to this land. You might be composing rengas,
 small verses:
about momentum
the widening that won't end
not when the plane lands

I write to you, now in Bolivia—tell you everything except how
 I admire
that you travel alone, that you aren't afraid to sleep under something
so large and unknown as the sky. By the time you get back to
 the States,
the other Amelia will have almost completed her journey around
the world; the cherry trees will be thick and green. It will have stopped
raining. I stand beneath my northern constellations—the
 moon tonight
in partial eclipse, the comet Hale-Bopp visible, tail streaming out
behind it in a journey of light—and hold out my two cupped hands,
thinking of the bowls in Machu Picchu—giving back to the sky
what it opened and let fall, traveling, to earth.

Inside

Where I work, packages arrive from India
at least once a week. Simple as nutshells,
the yellow padded envelopes are lined inside
with sheer cloth—patterned, embroidered,
stitched—remnant textiles or dresses, saris, cut
to size and sealed in the hems of parcels. We tear
open, peel the cloth away. How could we throw
out such gifts, such frayed remains? After visiting
Mt. St. Helens, someone tells me a story—
how when the mountain lost its face the sound
was heard miles away, but those at the volcano's
base, in its shadow and eye, heard nothing
at all—a quiet lifting. How the centers of things
surprise us—how, when we give things away,
we wrap them to make them more whole.

Cold
for the Russian submarine Kursk

It's summer, and I think of the men trapped
under 300 feet of Arctic ice, submarine
tipped into the ocean floor, one day of air
remaining. They must lie completely still,
breathe incredibly small breaths. They can
no longer tap on the hull; rescue efforts
move around them in the dark. And the sun
here is shining. Last night's moon was yellow
and low. Now the weeds in my garden
are not so urgent, my dog's paralyzed front leg
is not so sad. I love my husband even while
we argue. They will not live—all governments,
politics, miles of frozen sea. How can they
lie so still, when I am driving to work,
listening to the radio? Families in Russia
wake up cold, cannot sleep, and 300 feet
under the ice the world is quiet.
Shallow breaths lap against the dark.

Expectations

Listening to a performance of *Ivan the Terrible*
I am discovering that I do not much care for classical music—
even this Prokofiev with its inviting crescendos, even though
I try, even though my friend is singing in the choir. I do like
the narrator—his white and balding head, the way he grips
the music stand with both hands fisted. He is loud, perfect,
professional. And yet once, he stumbles over
a word, and this surprises me. His voice is supposed to be one
continuous boom. I try not to carry his mistake to the final
movement, but I find that I carry it all the way home.

It is the same with newscasters. I listen to NPR,
to the even-tempoed, enuniciated voices. I forget
they are human. The news should come to me in a steady
line of words, syllables whose s's don't hiss, whose t's
don't startle, whose k's don't catch in the back of the throat.
Today's forecast is rain, in one form or another, in every part
of the state. The woman reading the weather report slips
on her words halfway through, loses herself in the endless
repetition of thunderstorms, showers, partly cloudy, chance of rain.
I remember that her mind must wander as much
as mine does: she is thinking of the groceries to be bought
as she gives the extended forecast, of the woman with the red
umbrella she drove past this morning on her way to work
as she announces *This is Oregon Public Broadcasting, the
    news is next.*

At the coast two months ago, I was walking the water's frigid
edge with my friend—late night, dark skies. The only light
was the edge of each wave, long silver lines spreading and falling.
The shape hung before us as shadows did when I was a child—
the longer I stared into the darkness, the more I believed something
moved, something was there. But this shape was familiar,

a shape I carry engraved on my right shoulder—long neck, thin legs,
wings enough to hold the moon beneath them. But who expects
a heron standing in the waves, perfectly still, not rocked at all
as the tide comes in? Who expects such a bird to let you pass by,
unnoticed, as it stares out into the ocean, looking to where
    the moon
should be? I expected sound to matter. I expected flight.

Every morning I rub lotion into my detailed wound, reaching
awkwardly with my left arm to the bottom edge
of the tattoo, where the wings become the face
of a moon. I listen to the radio, telling me what the day
will be like. But when I walk outside and it isn't raining
after all, I remember that they cannot know what fills
this sky—the dark blue light, the conversations
of starlings, the unexpected folding of wings.

Aviary

It is like when I used to visit zoos,
pressing the large doors open
and stepping into the aviary—
humid creation of rain, dripping
like distant static, and all the hidden
voices calling at once. Trees tucked
under ceilings and into green tile walls,
me scanning for colors and wings.
Small sandpipers racing to locate a tide,
black-eyed birds making the crossing
from one side of the room to the other,
sure there is sky here somewhere, the visitors
must have come from somewhere. No wonder
there is so much noise. Today, I open
a window to let in cool air and discover
the backyard is singing, because
it is raining, and the sound floods
into my house—singing, because
it is raining, after forty-seven days
of no rain.

Crows

The telephone wires bend with crows, lining
the highways that travel to I am here you are there—
I imagine them sitting over roads as I dial the number
of a friend who has moved away, one of many
I try to hold on to with the reach of my voice.
Rooms around me have gone quiet—I think
the doors and windows might vanish, the walls might go,
and I will have to find some other way to define home.
A woman tells me about the Tower of London
where they clip the wings of crows to make them stay—
fearing if too many leave, the city will fall.
I want to hold them here, bring them back, gather
the stuff of nest building, admire wings from up close.
The line of sky is wide. The lines of crows
are long. They lift wings over roads and are everywhere,
                                                      everywhere.

St. Mark's Cathedral, Seattle

Nine-thirty tonight and the Episcopalian youth
sprawl themselves on the carpeted steps
before the altar; women and men who belong here
cross themselves as they move down the center
of the church like a bloodline. And I
curl my fingers together, guarding the triangle
of my pelvis, never having crossed myself
before, not even knowing which shoulder
comes first—my fingertips being more familiar
with the length of my hair, the lids of my eyes,
my breasts. I lower my head not in humility
or prayer, but out of inexperience and the weight
of uncomfortable silences. Sixteen-year old boys
sit with their arms on their knees,
their heads in their arms, looking
as if they carry the weight of all of America's
youth on their backs, and the voice
of the tenor rises, bells into this space—
the high ceilings, the arched windows, the open
doors. Once, in a Catholic church, I sat
with my sister while the Communion line
formed, feeling conspicuous as angels,
knowing the dryness of my body, the emptiness
of my mouth. I want to prop my feet
on the kneelers, know why the same sixteen-year old
who smokes behind the school between classes,
holds girls' breasts in the palms of his hands,
sits here looking like he knows something
I will never know, like he believes in the full drone
of the bass, the fine male harmonies, the murmured
words as ingrained as nursery rhymes. The choir
files out, robes gathered at the throats of old men, young men,

like the anticipation of a note between
pitch pipe and voice, and I unknit my fingers
to brush the hair from my face—the eyes
of the boys again raised upward, cast
into the world like a confession, or a song.

Sunday Mornings

He looks around, around, and he sees
angels in the architecture, spinning
in infinity, and he says 'amen' and 'hallelujah'.
   —Paul Simon

    I wait always for the bells
    from the church behind my house.
    They forgive
    the neighbors' yelling, the vacant house
    next door. Nine-thirty, they sound
    31 times. I'm still asking
    about the number, eliminating beads
    on the rosary, age when crucified. Maybe
    a verse, a psalm, the trinity plus one.
    Even the almost-priest doesn't know.
    This Sunday,
    after the bells, twin spires silent, two carved
    angels resting in stone—I hear singing.
    Faint—a small joy warming. I lean out
    my window to find it, see a man smiling up
    at me, waving. Waving back I pull my head in,
    move to find my husband, and the singing stops.
    The man vanishes. His song fades into children
    on the street. I am thinking of how
    my cat will die tomorrow—she's old, wasted
    down to bone. Of how the bells return
    every weekend. Of how the man
    is like a ghost, taken back to the low-income
    apartments, the market rushing trash into
    the street greens. One yellow tomcat
    in my yard watched by two angels.
    At any moment
    any of them could open into song.

Angels

The man at the watch counter watching us
says *I don't question how angels come to me*
we have chosen the watch
he didn't know he wanted
he wants one too calls us
angels I feel the nubs of wings turn
my eyes to him rough something
renegade leather torn edges
his partner thin more frail a watch
for him too two identical watches
identical to the one we've chosen
but do not buy I feel the nubs of wings
remember the flocking
sandhill cranes surprising us
among geese taller and voices
lifted the brown bodies walking
through wetland soft rain coming
in wind hundreds walking opening
wings and dancing calling
across cold spring afternoon
how often do we get to be angels
nothing to do with watches
with wings or not wings
two men buying identical watches
us turning away from timekeeping
I don't question how angels come

That Quickly

Near Colorado Springs
the highway bright
I picture my mother singing
in the car along with the music
some other woman's voice
her hand tapping the steering wheel
her left foot tapping lightly
her head moving slightly side to side
the car filled with music on the highway
an autumn Sunday afternoon
the car filled with the day's uprootings
small shoots of plants and herbs
tucked into new soil
making the journey to a new garden
my mother singing
the plants leaning lightly with the road
and then there is the truck
she drives beside it singing
in the blind spot
the truck does not see her singing
changes lanes right into my mother
in her purple singing car
thinks he has a blowout
does not see
as the car spins in front of the truck
my mother screams
the music forgotten
the driver's window pressed
against the grille and still
he does not see her
pushes her sideways
down the highway top speed
the yellow aspen the blue sky
and how the car does not buckle

and how she isn't pulled under
and how the newly potted plants
aren't overturned
no dirt anywhere inside the car
and how the truck finally slows and stops
sees my mother screaming
her car pushed sideways
a quarter mile down the highway
and how she gets out walking
the plants leaning out to watch her
whole
quivering
it can go that quickly
or find you walking
when it stops to rest.

Sky Falling

When he's late, you don't assume
he's stopped for milk
or is stuck behind a train.
Instead, you picture metal against metal,
slick streets and overturned cars,
sirens, the voice of the woman
from the hospital when she calls
to tell you the news.
You think about the sound you would make—
first silence, then an opening like blinding
light, collapsing into a slide of scree.
Which friend would you call first?
How would you get to the ER?
And afterward, would you give up
your life and move away
from everything?

You think of how the sun breaks
on the window of the church
behind your house, tumbles
down the walls into the street.
Conjure the scent of cigars and rain
as he curls around you from the cold side
of the bed. Wonder why you yell
at the dog when what you mean to do
is change the way you live.

So you're drawn to the disasters
in the news. The shipwrecks,
plane crashes, bombings. The story
of the ladies of Locherbie
collecting the clothes of the dead—
torn, bloodstained—how they washed
them as best they could, folding and pressing

each shirt, each dress, and returning
them to the families like sleeping ghosts.

When you can't sleep, you invent
what could happen. You imagine the pain.
You can't place it, it isn't yours. But you
hold it in your hands like a stone,
roll it over and over, feel the weight.
You can't imagine putting it down.

Your shoulders tighten like clouds before
a storm, the deep blue sky moving in.
But then he pulls into the drive, the dog
wakes and stirs, you hear the key in the lock.
And you're done imagining the woman
without a husband, the husband spinning
into this tree, that guardrail.
The ambulance, the helicopters,
the world a potential falling.

You're done.

Scotch Broom

To me, they will always be glorious birds.
—*Maude, from* Harold and Maude *by Colin Higgins*

Just when people seem to be falling away from me
like stars too old to hold on to the sky any longer,
the daffodils are opening their mouths into the grey
spring light of this city with its small rain, its wide
belly of clouds, and I wonder how they can do this beautiful
thing without the sun to raise their hopes and warm
their heavy faces. It was two years ago I was driving
to the coast and first saw the yellow flush lining
the highway, asked a local what it was: Scotch broom—
a weed, a determined, spreading bush—but like Maude
and her seagulls, I was thinking, *to me they will always
be glorious birds*, this full brave yellow that hides
the clearcuts, the grass just back from a fire, the eggs
of birds who make their nests in the ground.

And I wished for Scotch broom in my own backyard,
for jade plants which a friend insisted were a nuisance
in California, nothing of value, something to be uprooted
to make room for smaller, more colorful flowers. I wished
for my world to become an easier place, where the people
I gathered around me would spin together like vines,
tangle themselves about me like the morning glories
on the fence of the house I lived in when I was five—
the slender lengths curled in and out of each other
and into the neighbors' yard, the neighbors who wanted
us to tear down this quick weed and its white cups
of flowers with their inner surprise of blue
waking each morning and folding to sleep each night
as I do now, waiting for the season to change.

My hands are full of small eggs, small flowers,
delicate hope. What of this is ordinary?
It is people who create constellations, not the stars

who die long before we will ever realize they are gone.
I am thinking of the highway to the coast, of two years
ago when my arms could hold everyone at once,
nested. When did these relationships change so wildly,
grow out of my hands, cease to be beautiful? I know
I am close to the ocean when the seagulls come
in pairs, then in threes, then in whole families of wings,
when Scotch broom gives way to sand—
to sand and the long reaching of a landscape where
things arrive, stay barely long enough to be discovered,
and are taken back, slip under, fall away.

In The Name

In downtown Portland, the gate to Old Town
doesn't lead to incensed shops, sweet-smelling groceries,
or restaurants whose doors open onto slender chopsticks,
snow peas, and handleless teacups. The two open-mouthed lions
turn their backs to the lit signs, the windowless store fronts,
the heavy doors. When I was first old enough to ask
how I was named, *Playboy* was a rabbit's head
on a swizzle stick, a stack of boxes in my grandfather's
basement. It wasn't triple x, this man sitting on the sidewalk,
this street where I won't walk alone.

When my mother told me I was named after
a *Playboy* bunny, I thought of Easter. I thought of Kenny,
the boy down the block who had a rabbit, who was two years
older than me, whose house I biked to while my heart beat
into ribbons when I found the rabbit hit by a car. Or Patrick,
who in fourth grade showed me his penis in my garage
as if it were some strange bird, a Darwinian finch. I told
all my friends where my name came from, reveled in its
peculiar spelling, argued with the boy in first grade
who insisted it had three syllables instead of two.

It was a year ago I was talked into looking her up
in the used bookstore with its aisles of periodicals, just
six blocks from the gate and its lions. I could not turn
the pages, thinking of coming to Portland for college,
how in my first year the Women's Center sponsored a lecture
on pornography—slides of women bound, women's breasts roped
off and noosed, a Chinese woman holding an erect penis, her face
pained, eyes closed, mouth twisted, her lips parted and spilling
white drops like tears down her chin. My friend found her
in the lower right-hand corner of a page, elbows rising
to lift her shirt over her head, the shirt pausing between
belly and breasts, my first name printed below her hips.

A friend learning Gaelic once told me that my last name
means fairy, elf, something magical. When I told my father,
he said he'd always thought it meant courage. I remember this
when my grandfather sells the first year's issues of his *Playboy*s,
when I walk past the lions with their open mouths and
    still tongues,
when my lips work their way down my lover's belly to the space
between his hips, when I tell someone the story of my name.

Massage

Two rooms away from you, I look out
onto a garden—tomato vines
blackened in their cages, rain
shuddering calla lilies twice the size
of my own. I hear the drift of music,
soft exchange of voices as another woman
touches you, works to heal the pain in your back.

This week, we have forgotten to be patient
with each other. Forgotten about sleeping
in the curves of each other's spines. How small
words have been placed between us, too slippery
to pick up. The weather today makes
wind chimes clatter with urgency—
we are reluctant to step outside.

I anticipate driving you home, inhaling
scent of oil from your skin. The roads
will be slick and flooded, the day will be turning
dark. Your eyes will be closed, hands
calm in your lap. Tonight, I will lie curled
around your back, still scented with oil—
a single touch will turn us to rain.

Window

Something about the moonlight through the slats
of our bed, that we don't have curtains
for the windows. And though the house
on one side is vacant, the blinds on the other side
drawn, someone might see. It's a kind
of rush, like we're a black and white film—
silent—guests in the house. Our mouths
forming quiet Os, lit with moonlight,
a leader of film ticking crazily into movement,
picture, person. If I take you in my hands,
coax you forward against me, your silhouette
will arch, sigh a long silent breath.
You will mark my left breast in silence,
and I'll notice the light on your shoulders,
casting of shadow and skin. The world will be
sleeping, the very air sleeping, but we'll imagine
quick changes of light—a cracked blind,
an open window, a baby waking.
Rhythmic return of a film rolling back
to itself—light cast on a quiet room, my nipples
rimmed upwards, your hand falling still
above your head—and everywhere a rising,
moving into a lit room of sleep.

How We Come Home

What we gather instead of sticks or wayward twists
of fabric are pine boards to build bookshelves, broad-leaved
plants, photographs, the softest flannel sheets. We lean
toward silvery cookware the way crows bee-line
for every simple, shiny thing. Crocuses are blooming
on the side of the house, where we didn't know
there were crocuses. Long, green daffodil leaves
surprise us in the yard—someone else planted them before
we moved in. And you—you are wearing new glasses,
your body is quieter than before. In the mornings, I feed
the new dog. It has rained for so many days in a row.

Wandering albatross partner for life, then live apart for months
at a time. Greeting each other after days of solitary wind,
they mimic each other in flight, a wing turning sideways
invites the other's wing. The longest lengths of feathers and bone
are perfectly matched, synchronized in the celebration of return.
Sometimes we feel like this at the end of a day, many long
hours of separate dailiness. Cooking dinner is my shoulders
bending to chop vegetables, your hands reaching for the oil.
Making love is first your belly to my back, your pelvis tipped
perfectly to balance my hips, then our shoulders and collarbones
matching, our arms stretched out together, palm to palm, like wings.

The wind knocks out our power and I light candles in every room,
even though it is almost time for bed. The house is larger this way,
the faces of our cats silhouetted and looking back at me, every
humming thing gone quiet. The astronomers have taken
Pluto out of the solar system. It tricked them into believing
it was a real planet, more than tightly spinning dust. But it belonged
for so long, and we have never even visited, though we talk of it
like the house down the block. I say let us keep it. We have given
it a name. It is part of how we find our way home. And as for us,
we are keeping track of the stars through our kitchen window.
We are building nest after nest. Kindling light after light.

ABOUT THE AUTHOR

Brittney Corrigan was raised in Colorado but has called Portland, Oregon her home since 1990. She holds a degree from Reed College, where she is also employed. She is the poetry editor for the online journal *Hyperlexia: poetry and prose about the autism spectrum*. Brittney's poems have appeared in numerous journals and anthologies, and she is also the author of the chapbook, *40 Weeks*, published by Finishing Line Press. She lives with her husband Thomas and their two children. For more information, visit Brittney's website: http://brittneycorrigan.com/.

Photo: Serena Davidson